CW00375416

Life in the RAF

Photon Books

Life in the RAF

An erk's-eye view

Geoff (Ginge) Dann

Photonbooks
www.photonbooks.com

Published by Photon Books
First published in Great Britain in 2010
www.photonbooks.com

Printed and bound in Great Britain by
Imprint Digital, Exeter

ISBN 978-906420-10-9

Vickers Valiant

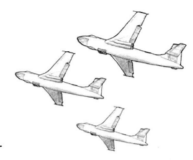

During the 1950's and 60's through the height of the cold war the role of nuclear deterrent fell to the RAF in the shape of the V-force. The trio of Valiant, Victor and Vulcan all saw service using conventional weapons but only the Valiant was to deliver a nuclear weapon, as part of development trials. Retired early when a switch to low-level operations led to fatigue problems, the Valiant has slipped farthest from the memory.

Funds raised by the sale of this book will be used to support the establishment of a museum exhibit dedicated to ensuring the story of the Vickers Valiant is kept alive.

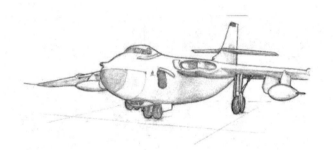

Foreword

Formed in 2003, 'Friends of 138 Valiant Squadron' is a group of geriatric teenagers all of whom worked on or flew the Vickers Valiant in the RAF. As the founder and motivating force of this group it is my great pleasure to say a few words by way of introduction to this collection of cartoons created by our talented group member Geoff Dann.

Through these pages you can glimpse Geoff's take on the 'Life of an Erk' in the RAF drawn from memories of the group now stretching back over half a century. You will also see a little of the activities of the group in the much more recent past. I'd like to take a moment to mention these more recent exploits.

In 2008 we attempted to obtain the cabin from a Vickers Valiant which would then be transported to Thorpe Camp in Lincolnshire to be placed on display. Unfortunately the plans for this fell through but did provide a rich vein of 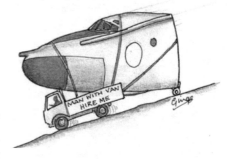 inspiration for Geoff. Additionally the money collected for the project provided the impetus to create a commemorative Valiant Museum at Thorpe Camp. This project is now underway and money raised through the sales of this book will help establish this unique memorial to the first of the V-Bombers.

In September 2008 it was announced that HRH Prince William had been appointed Honorary Air Commodore at Thorpe Camp's near neighbour, RAF Coningsby. I wrote to Prince William extending the offer of honorary membership of Friends of 138 Valiant Squadron. Despite having to decline our invitation, the response from Clarence House will take its place amongst 'The Friends' collection and provided yet more cartoon ideas.

I hope you enjoy these cartoons and I would like to take this opportunity to thank you wholeheartedly for your support.

Robin (Nobby) Unwin (Huthwaite) September 2009

Find out more about the Vickers Valiant, the activities of The Friends and progress at Thorpe Camp by visiting. www.valiants-r-us.co.uk.

cartoons by Ginge.

Ginge

Where's the bloody Naafi Wagon?
I'm fair clemmed!

Ginge's cartoons began in 2005 during the early days of *'Friends of 138 Squadron'*. His inspiration has often come from the nostalgic atmosphere of the *Friends'* frequent reunions, thriving on the cheery banter, the overheard anecdotes and the hilarious reminiscences of the one-time *erk*. In this book you will find two collections of Ginge's work.

In Part 1 the fictional erk Jacka Orltrades looks back on life in the RAF almost fifty years ago. Jacka is a blend of the immortal war-time 'Pilot Officer Prune' and the mythical 'Kilroy', who seemed to get everywhere. With a basis in fact and a sprinkling of artistic licence, his exploits are a pictorial write-up of events... some true and others rather fanciful.

In a second collection of cartoons the trials, tribulations and undoubted successes of 'Friends of 138 Squadron' chart the exploits of this group of ex servicemen and their determination to keep alive the memory of the Vickers Valiant, the first, but sadly most neglected, of the RAF's V-Bombers.

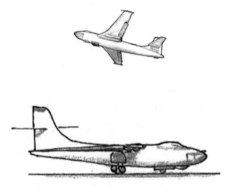

'The life of an erk.'

Jacka Orltrades echoes the spirit of Pilot Officer Prune and the ubiquitous Kilroy. Here we follow the daily life of an RAF erk. Perhaps these incidents will rekindle memories of events you witnessed, were told of, or maybe were even involved in.

18 yrs old .... and Ma Orltrades' little lad Jacka joins 'the mob'.

Hey, Ma!
They've called me up.

Reckon Oi'll 'ave
ter give up me
paper round.

Thort Oi
wuz gonna
be a
"Brylcreem
Boy".

Wodjer mean, "Mister"?
Them's stripes, so it's Corporal" ter you!!

.... 'an do somethin' 'wi'
that stupid bloody
beret!!

It don' work Corperil

There mus' be one
stuck in t' spout.

From day 1, Jacka tried very hard to please everybody. He really was very trying.

Pay Parade .. Jacka was not very good with numbers

Er ... can Oi just 'ave a quick look at me 1251?

We've all seen it happen and tried not to smirk with satisfaction, knowing that our own £1.8s was safely in a tunic pocket along with our 1250. I did a 'Jacka' at West Kirby and Cpl, Conway had me reciting my full RAF number AND my 1250 number about a dozen times a day until next pay parade. 5027762 ... A204506. They're still there after 50 years.. But I can't remember my own phone number.

Square bashing in winter at West Kirby

That man!!
Get some coal and some firewood and light that stove.

Right!

Where'd you get the wood, then?

Well, I found some brooms in the store-room, so I just broke 'em up.
Come an' 'ave a warm- up, Corp.

Light a fire?
Doesn't sound like the West Kirby I remember. ......
Certainly not Smuts Squadron!

Every ex-RAF serviceman has a special memory from Square-bashing days.

Scene: Towards end of square-bashing, on Smuts Sqdn, RAF West Kirby, Sept. 1956.

Sprog, en-route to NAAfI & deep in thought, fails to salute Officer in company of SWO.

THAT MAN!!

After whipping off a smart salute and an apology to the Officer, sprog aborts visit to NAAFI and makes a hasty return to billet for change of underpants!

"NULLO MODO VINCES" .... Who says so?

Jacka on SWO's working party. Jacka thought he looked good in denim overalls, which was just as well really, as he was to spend a lot of his time on fatigues... usually in the Cookhouse tin room or pushing a broom.

Jacka Orltrades .... Always ready to help

On 13/09/1957, Valiant WZ398 exploded in a hangar at RAF Wyton. The external electrical power supply had been connected while work on the fuel tanks was in progress.

Jacka Orltrades .... you knew 'im!

'Ere y' go, Jacka. Chiefy wants yer ter top up the nosewheel tyres on our kite.
'E says a coupla pounds should do it.

Ee, I've got one o' them at 'ome on me trade-bike wot I used ter use when I did me paper round, afore I got me call-up.

I 'ad a spot o' bother wi' the ol' bike pump, so I got me mate from the AA to bring 'is kit an' do the job.

Oh, an' 'e says to let Chiefy know the tread's nearly down to the canvas.

"Me Mam always swears by a bit o' Daz down the ol' pan, but I reckon it'll take a whole packet to do the works on the bogs in this block! "

"I am not amused ..... but since you find it so funny Airman, you can get this lot cleaned up right away.

See to it, Sergeant!"

BILLET INSPECTION

Jacka Orltrades .... Chiefy's worst nightmare

Hey Chiefy!
'S OK.   Oi found me toolbag.
Oi musta left it up the jet pipe.

Typical Jacka ... but do you remember breaking into a cold sweat when you were on the kite's wing, watching a screwdriver rolling down towards flaps or aileron?

Jacka Orltrades ..... Fairy

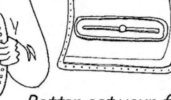

Cor, Sarge! Lookit orl them screws. Thass gonner take orl day.

Better get your finger out and get started fixin' it then, Orltrades!

There ain't enuff 'oles, Sarge. I gotter 'and full o' screws left over.

Woddy 'ell d'yer mean ? Get it sorted, y' dozy bugger!

Jacka Orltrades ..... Rigger's mate.

AC2 Orltrades J. .... remustered.

Lookit me Ma!
Tug Driver!
This is gonna be the fastest Compass Swing ever!
Just watch me go .... YEE HAAAA

Jacka Orltrades .... Armourer's Mate.

New sprint records were set the day Jacka improvised when he couldn't find a bomb trolley.

AT LAST IT CAN BE TOLD.......
Who was it who pulled the handle to fire the canopy explosive bolts instead of the brake handle when the tug stopped?

It weren't me Chief! It was that daft bugger Orltrades back there in the driver's seat!

WAS IT JACKA ORLTRADES WOT DONE IT?
            Ask Charlie Dunmore & Sam Brooksbank!

Jacka was in his element in the Cookhouse ... usually in the Tin Room!

WISHING YOU A MERRY CHRISTMAS
.... AND A HAPPY NEW YEAR

Here's hoping Cookhouse Fatigues
....and the dreaded Tin Room....
are not too heavy this Christmas

Ginge

Freezing cold Sunday night. Train late into P'boro East. Legged it to P'boro N. but missed the gang who usually shared taxi to Wittering.

Go get y'r head down in the Porter's Room, Sunshine. Y'll freeze y'r cobs off out 'ere.

I'll give yer a shout when y'r mates arrive off the London train.

Wakey, wakey Lad!

London train's in and some o' y'r mates are lookin' for one more f'r a taxi load.

36

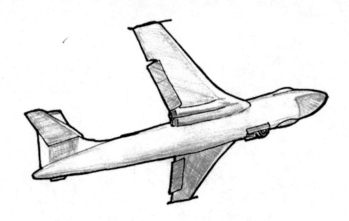

"BURN THE F700"

DECEMBER 1957. The first a/c flies after RAF Honington's Valiant Major Servicing Flight's 3 month task. The nosewheel failed to retract but, since it was virtually in circuit for its destination (RAF Watton) as soon as it had 'cleared the fence', it did not return to Honington. The fault was attributed to a missing fuse!

VSF Major was disbanded after the second a/c in March 1958.

PAY DAY ... AND THE LATE NIGHT CARD-SCHOOL.   Nowt like it to stop the rest of the billet getting a bit o' kip.

Card sharps are still out at the Malcolm or in Stamford, tanking up.

Them as are ready to turn in 'ave a cunning plan!

Billet lights off and put piece of ally foil from fag packet in bulb-holder.
Replace bulb.
Everyone in pit and heads down.

Wallies return, all fired up and ready for noisy card school until small hours. 1st bloke hits switch ... there is a flash as lights fuse. Much swearing as trip is re-set but repeatedly blows again.
They decide they can't be bothered, so with a lot of stamping around they hit the sack.   **"G'night lads!"**

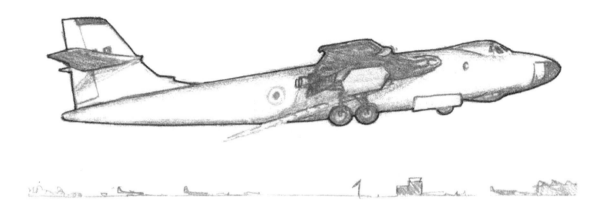

August '58 …. RATOG trials with 138 Sqdn.

Jettisoning the Super Sprite units ….

…. the theory

…. the problem

.... the outcome

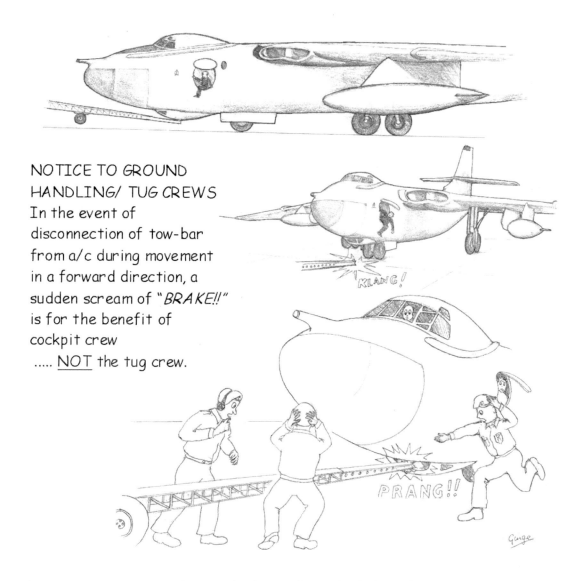

NOTICE TO GROUND
HANDLING/ TUG CREWS
In the event of
disconnection of tow-bar
from a/c during movement
in a forward direction, a
sudden scream of "*BRAKE!!*"
is for the benefit of
cockpit crew
..... <u>NOT</u> the tug crew.

Oops. Who was it dropped an almighty clanger?

THE RELUCTANT VALIANT 'JOCKEY'

BUT CHIEF,
I.......

OK DONNELLY—WE'VE GOT A TOW TO
VSF HANGAR..... AND YOU'RE GONNA
HAVE TO STEER THE KITE.
Y'JUST HAVE TO CRANK THE WHEEL.
— I'LL SHOW YOU.   NO BUTS!!

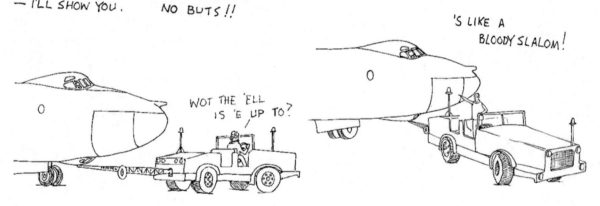

WOT THE 'ELL
IS 'E UP TO?

'S LIKE A
BLOODY SLALOM!

It was a fairly steep learning curve when you were new to the squadron...
particularly if you had made the mistake of showing a bit of initiative at
some time. One did one's best.

"BOMBEX"

04:00 THE DUTY MECH.
RECKONS HE'S
EARNED
AN EARLY
BREAKFAST

04:10
A CLOSE
ENCOUNTER
WITH A "CANNY" ON THE PERI-TRACK.

EARLY BREAKFAST??

YOU MUST BE
JOKIN' MATE!

NOWT LEFT.... AN'
I'M JUST DRINKIN'
THE LAST O' THE
BREW.

COME BACK
AT 07:00

'ERE Y'ARE TED.
..... 5 SUGARS

TED'S
TANKARD

DUTY CREW
LAST NIGHT.
DO NOT
DISTURB.

08:00,   AND A
REAL MUCKER BRINGS THAT
MAGIC MUG OF TEA.

Chaz insists the drawing doesn't come anywhere near to doing justice to the speed at which he left the jet pipe. He says that his feet barely touched the ground.

The Ballad of WZ402

'twas April 1st at Witt'ring.
  On the jet pan stood 402.
Bill Craze and 'is mates 'ad been up all night.
  .... It's tough bein' Duty Crew.

When the kite gave a sigh of exhaustion.
  "I've 'ad a late night", said she.
As she folded up 'er nosewheel
  and went down on bended knee.

Bill shouted the news to Chiefy
  Who thought 'twas an April Fool joke.
"Piss off, y' daft bugger", said Chiefy,
  For 'e was that sort of bloke.

But when Bill got to convince 'im
  to go out and 'ave a quick look,
'e was totally dumb and 'is beret fell off.
  Y'might say 'e was visibly shook.

"Don't panic, Boys", 'e said, panicking ....
  As they tied the main gear up with rope.
Not that that would've done any good
  But you can always live in hope.

If the main gear 'ad powered into action,
  They might just as well tied 'em wi' string
But luckily nothing more 'appened.
  402 was soon back on the wing. Ginge

wot's wrong with a lady takin'
a nap after a night on the tiles?

Friends of 138

From the germ of an idea in 2005, Friends of 138 Valiant Squadron has grown to a membership of well over 50, veterans who meet regularly to share old memories and create a few new ones. Their shared passion is the Vickers Valiant and the determination that the first of the Cold-War V-Bombers should not be forgotten.

Nobby's Dream

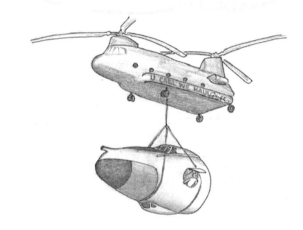

D eep in darkest Huthwaite there stirs a plan to transport the nose section of the last Valiant ever built back to a home in Lincolnshire bomber country by any means possible. Here it will form the centre piece of a Valiant memorial and museum.

NOBBY'S DREAM .... How do we get from Inverness to Lincolnshire?

Four an' twenty Valiant men went up to Inverness .....
an' when the Ball was over the Scots 'ad a Valiant less!
Singin' .... Who was it nicked it? Who 'ad it away?
'Twas just the lads of 138 an' 'ere it's goin' to stay!

COMING HOME TO LINCOLNSHIRE

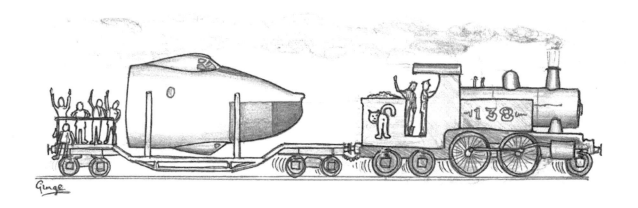

NOT EXACTLY THE FLYING SCOTSMAN..... BUT A VALIANT EFFORT

"Eight Seven Five Special's comin' down the track.
Been to Scotland, comin' back......" (Six-Five Special)

INVERNESS → MORAY FIRTH → NORTH SEA → THE WASH → BOSTON

Have you lost us Navigator?
Come up here and take a look.
Someone's shot our ruddy tail off.

Never mind.   There's Donna Nook!

"Clementine"

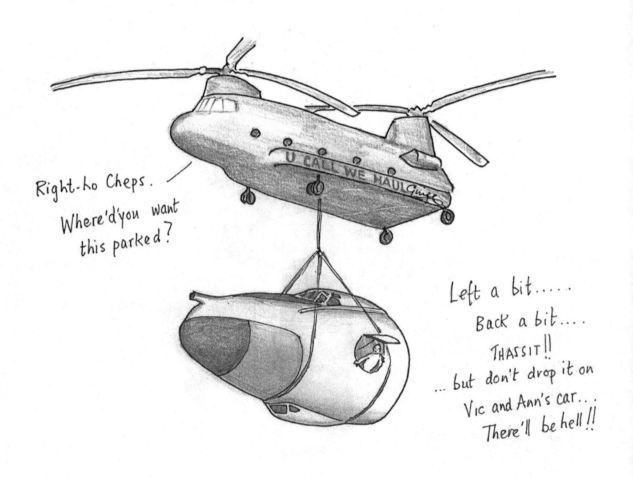

58

Oops!   I Hope he's got some decent brakes!

"Speed bonny boat, like a bird on the wing ......"

INVERNESS → CALEDONIAN CANAL → IRISH SEA →
MERSEYSIDE → M62 → A1 → LINCOLNSHIRE

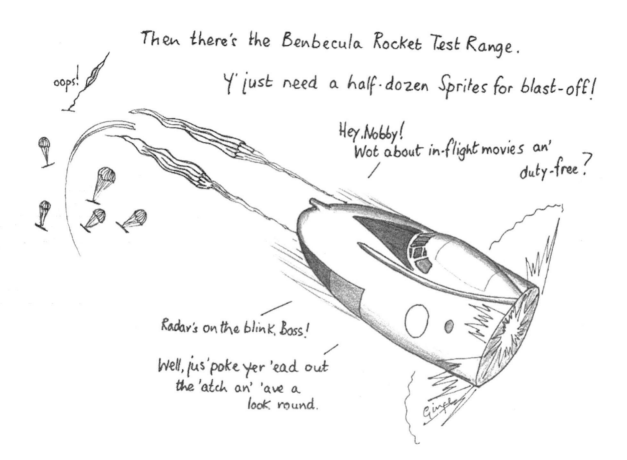

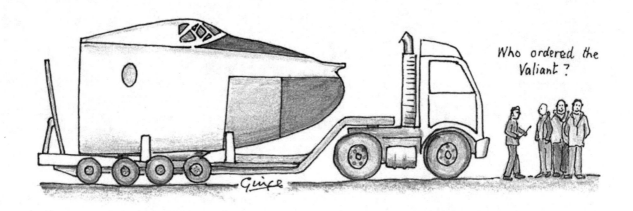

GREAT.... BUT JUST IMAGINE .... ON A 'QUEEN MARY' TRAILER!

THE ROYAL VISITOR

THORPE CAMP
INCORPORATING
VALIANT
COMMEMORATIVE
MUSEUM

ORLTRADES
DODGY DEALS

Ginge

Me an' my mate Lofty Shortplank
'eard y'wuz still lookin' fer a Valiant
cabin. So..... we went up t' Cosford
an' jus' hacked it orf. Told 'em it
wuz due fer Major Servicin'.

Jacka goes through civvy life in much the same way he ambled through his time in the RAF, before they got tired of him. Typical Orltrades, this 'dodgy deal' came complete with a large drum of 'auntie flash paint', as he called it, and "a coupla undercarriage 'D' doors they wasn't usin' prop'ly."

Valiant Reborn

Simon Steggall... a Valiant enthusiast whose determination to build and fly a large-scale Valiant model has inspired and excited all who knew the real thing in the 1950's and 60's.

Bloody 'ell! It may be only ⅐ full-size but she's just as noisy as the real thing an' she don't 'arf go! Ginge

Simon is not merely a dreamer but has brought to reality the sight of an amazingly authentic flying Valiant.

He is also busy leading a team involved with the servicing and maintenance of a Second World War Hurricane, widely seen at air shows and displays.

RAF Wittering, 6th July 2005. A very proud and emotional day for Friends of 138 Valiant Squadron. Their reunion celebrated the 50th anniversary of the arrival at Wittering of 138 as the first V-Bomber squadron.

Ray Jones, Tony Skerrit, Simon (Chiefy) Steggall, Bill Meadows, Nobby Unwin, Tubbs Priest and Ginge Dann at Bentwaters in Suffolk on 30th July 2006. A spine-tingling experience for those who were privileged to see (and hear!) Simon's 5-metre wing span, turbojet powered Valiant in flight during its trials for certification for public display.

Simon's next project?   114ft span .... 4 x R.R. Avons

That sounds rather familiar, doesn't it?

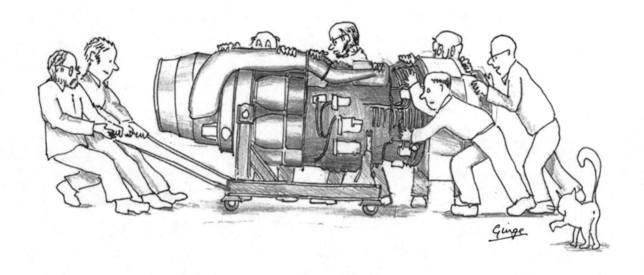

"Nobby says he wants us to park it over there, by Simon's van."

"If Nobby isn't careful, I'll show him just where we'll park it!"

Sorry about the heavy landing, Chaps.
Chiefy and Ground Crew are going to be miffed.
I think we may have burst a tyre.

There is a fragment of Valiant XD857 at the Norfolk and Suffolk Aviation Museum, Flixton.

'Nobby'

"I have nothing to offer but blood, toil, tears, sweat and ....
sausage rolls"

The inspirational efforts of Nobby our 'Senior Man' and founder of Friends of 138 Valiant Squadron ensure that the group's reunions are attended with great enthusiasm. His cheery reminders to get accommodation booked and to wear the tee-shirt, together with the promise of his spicy sausage rolls, keep us all on our toes.

Right, 138!
Orf yer pits an' get fell in!

Hope to see you soon.
138 Tee Shirts will
be worn......
and pots carried!

WOT THE 'ELL
IS THAT?

WELL, SARGE........
NOBBY'S ORDER WAS
"TEE-SHIRTS
WILL BE WORN".

NOBBY SAYS "DON'T PROCRASTINATE"—

WOSSAT?

OI WISH HE WUNT USE BIG WORDS —
THEY MAKE MOI BRAIN HURT.
SPOSE OI C'D GO AN' LOOK IT UP —
NAH! OI'LL WAIT 'TIL TERMORRER.

**FIRE PICKET?
GUARD DUTY?
CAN'T KEEP AWAKE?**

TRY
NOBBY'S LITTLE
HELPERS —

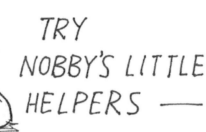

SPICY HUTHWAITE DOG ROLLS

They'll clear your sinuses
and blow your socks off !!

50 Years on, it can be revealed "The Beast"

was stuffed full of Nobby's sausage rolls!

ONE HELLUVA WEAPON

A Valiant ex-airman named Nobby
Took up running a website f'r a hobby.
  'Twas a brilliant success
  But he got in a mess
When he dumped all the contents
an' the 'Crewroom' went down the
plug 'ole an' by 'eck the air
were blue!!

But he's still a lot better at it than
I am at writing limericks!

Ginge

"TWAS CHRISTMAS DAY IN THE COOKHOUSE.... AND CPL. COOK McGREW
WAS SERVIN' UP CHRISTMAS PUDDIN'.... ALONG WITH THE FESTIVE STEW.
WHEN UP SPOKE A VALIANT AIRMAN.... IN A VOICE AS BOLD AS BRASS.
"WE DON'T WANT YOUR PUDDIN'.... YOU CAN GIVE IT TO THE POOR STARVIN'
LITTLE DICKYBIRDS".

"Only jokin', Cookie! A Merry Christmas to All".

" ..... and coffee will be served in the Officers' Mess"

Naughty, naughty, Gentlemen!
Removing the odd souvenir teaspoon is one thing .....
but furniture and fittings? A bit over the top, what?

It was during a visit by Friends of 138 Valiant Squadron to their old station at RAF Witering, that Michael Rondot's wonderful painting of a Valiant take-off was discovered... and coveted.

Simon   Trevor   Alf   Charlie   Tony   Vic   Brian

Ginge   Ray   Jim   Nobby   Pete   Taff   Ann

Friends of 138 Valiant Squadron at RAF MARHAM. 26th June 2008

It was an excellent visit and we needed no encouragement to pose for a photograph in front of a Tornado. A very proud moment... and big smiles We just pretended that it was 1960 and we were standing in front of a 138 Squadron Valiant.

50 YEARS ON.... TIME FOR THE ANNUAL FLU JAB BRINGS ON A SQUARE-BASHING FLASHBACK.

Not a lot has changed. You queue up with your coat over your arm and your shirt sleeve rolled up. There's a bit of nervous banter with your fellow victims. Then it's your turn and you stroll up and stand there, trying to look nonchalant and hoping it really won't hurt like it did last year.

Geoff Dann

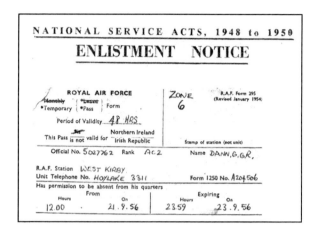

After months of boredom in the Wireless Section at Wittering, relief came when in my absence on leave I was 'volunteered' for a six month detachment at Honington in deepest Suffolk, my home county. 'Put Ginge's name down he's a Swede,.... that'll suit him down to the ground', So off to join Valiant Major Servicing Flight being set up to see what could be done 'in house' ... so to speak. At Honington I met Les Harrison, a cheery lad from Leeds on detachment from Marham. We became great pals as between us we saw out the modest and not over demanding tasks that our trade involved. Time dragged a bit as only two Valiants underwent the Major Servicing programme. We were at least involved 'hands-on' with the aircraft and on my return to Wittering I begged and pleaded my way onto a squadron.

On 138 Squadron (B flight) I spent the most satisfying months of my National Service. It was gratifying to feel that one's efforts were directed as part of a team towards something worthwhile. I was fortunate that these were the Spring and Summer months of '58. My abiding memories after fifty years are of warm summer days on B flight dispersal or stumbling from the smoky crew room in the small hours, shaking the sleep from our eyes. We would be met by the howls of a dozen Avon engines as our kites came rolling onto the jet pan after *Bombex*

sorties. There was the scramble to get 'after-flight' checks done and signed off, then leg it down to the mess for a brew (or maybe an early breakfast) and back to the billet for a kip until midday.

There were less rosy times of course and

little did most of us realise just how serious and 'heavy-duty' were the years of the cold war, of which our service days were part.

The memories of the camaraderie there was among the 'Erks' of 138 Squadron can still make me smile... just as I do when I reflect on the enjoyment of our reunions as 'Friends of 138 Valiant Squadron'.

Despite Paddy's threat, I did get demobbed on time.

Sah!! 762!!

Celebrating 50 years since Demob.
August 13th 1958

SAC Dann G.

Used to answer to nickname *"Ginge"*

91

With grateful thanks to the following who helped make this book possible.

Robin (Nobby) Unwin

Charlie Knight

Vic and Ann Savage

Tony Fellows

Collin (Heiny) Brown

Phil Holden

Steve (Paddy) Roe

Charlie Cunningham

Bernard Burgess

Gordon Geddes

Peter Rogers

Arthur Priest

Bill Craze

Les Harrison

Len Baker

Denis Mills

Tony Skerritt

Ray Jones

Bill Donnelly

Simon Steggall

Steve Short

Ken Bruce

Fred Best

Cliff Long

Bill Smith

Tony Fowler

Brian (Dick) Dickinson

Bill Meadows

FRIENDS OF 138

VALIANT SQUADRON

NULLO MODO VINCES

ATE Rev 3.0